Alexander Taggart McGill

American slavery

As viewed and acted on by the Presbyterian church in the United States of
America

Alexander Taggart McGill

American slavery
As viewed and acted on by the Presbyterian church in the United States of America

ISBN/EAN: 9783744736251

Printed in Europe, USA, Canada, Australia, Japan

Cover: Foto ©Suzi / pixelio.de

More available books at **www.hansebooks.com**

AMERICAN SLAVERY,

AS VIEWED AND ACTED ON

BY THE

PRESBYTERIAN CHURCH

IN THE

UNITED STATES OF AMERICA.

COMPILED FOR THE BOARD OF PUBLICATION,

BY THE

REV. A. T. McGILL, D.D.,

STATED CLERK OF THE GENERAL ASSEMBLY.

PHILADELPHIA:
PRESBYTERIAN BOARD OF PUBLICATION,
No. 821 CHESTNUT STREET.

AMERICAN SLAVERY.

For more than a century, after its introduction, slavery seems to have been accepted as a fact, in the social and civil condition of this country, which the Presbyterian church was called to consider with careful enlightenment, rather than hasty legislation; in view of her mission, to expound and apply great principles, before she ventured upon the enforcement of discipline. Accordingly, from the beginning, her utterances on the subject have been mature, comprehensive, and consistent. There is not one deliverance, to be found on record, which we would suppress or conceal. It is true, that, in seeking to moderate the rage of human passions, and guard against fanatical extremes, she has met this and that prevailing agitation, with special forms of declaration, that some have reproached as departure from earlier and more formal enunciation of principles: but they only need to be brought into one connected view, in the light of different times, and the changing circumstances which evoked them, to appear all, but varying aspects of the same determination.

3

Four things are always to be discerned, clearly, in the result aimed at, as often as this church has been brought to express her mind, respecting slavery in our land. 1st. The ultimate emancipation of the slave, and overthrow of the whole system as an evil thing. 2d. The amelioration of the system while it lasts, by subjecting to her watchful discipline the relation of master and slave. 3d. The religious education of slaves and their children, to fit them for the enjoyment of liberty, as well as to save their souls. 4th. The use of regenerated black men as an instrumentality for the evangelization of Africa; which white men cannot achieve, by reason of its climate.

I. It is singular, that this last object, and apparently the most remote and incidental, was the first to engage the action of our church; so far as the record evinces. Dr. Samuel Hopkins, pastor at Newport, R. I., a pupil and biographer of Jonathan Edwards; distinguished in theology as the author of the "Hopkinsian system;" was probably the first man in our country, to stir up an organized political action against slavery—succeeding, in 1774, to obtain the passage of a law, prohibiting the importation of slaves into the colony. In the previous year, 1773, he had formed a plan for evangelizing Africa, by sending negro missionaries, duly qualified: and had enlisted the zealous co-operation of Dr. Ezra Stiles, pastor of another church in Newport, and subsequently, the learned and eminent President of Yale College. Those two ministers communicated their project, by formal overture, to the Synod of New York and Philadelphia, met at Philadelphia, May, 1774. The ready interest on which they counted, was manifested in the character of the Committee, appointed to report on the overture—consisting of men who were famous in their day for patriotism and philanthropy. All the items gleaned from our Minutes, pp. 456—8, are as follows:

"A representation from the Rev. Dr. Ezra Stiles and the Rev. Samuel Hopkins, respecting the sending two natives of Africa on a mission to propagate Christianity in their native country, and a request that the Synod would countenance this undertaking by their approbation of it, was brought in and read."

"The representation and request relative to sending negro missionaries to Africa, was taken into consideration, in consequence of which the subject of negro slavery came to be considered, and after much reasoning on the matter Dr. Rodgers, Messrs. John Miller, Caldwell, and Montgomery, were appointed a committee to bring in an overture on this subject on Wednesday morning."

"The committee appointed to prepare an overture on the representation from Dr. Stiles and the Rev. Samuel Hopkins, and also on the subject of negro slavery, brought in a draught, the first part of which being read and amended, was approved, and is as follows:

"The Synod is very happy to have an opportunity to express their readiness to concur with and assist in a mission to the African tribes, and especially where so many circumstances concur, as in the present case, to intimate that it is the will of God, and to encourage us to hope for success. We assure the gentlemen aforesaid, we are ready to do all that is proper for us in our station for their encouragement and assistance."

1 *

"But some difficulties attending the discussion of the second part of that overture, the Synod agree to defer the affair to our next meeting."—*Minutes*, 1774, pp. 456, 458.

The confusion of the country, (as it was now approaching the struggle with Great Britain for independence, in an early stage of which, the Newport pastors and people were dispersed, and the projects of benevolence set aside, by the calamities of invasion and war,) must account for the entire silence of our courts, in their subsequent meetings, respecting this interesting enterprise.

II. The *second* record on the subject of slavery, made May 28th, 1787, *avowed distinctly the ultimate emancipation of the slaves as the policy of the church.* This may be called the first *action* on the subject, declarative of principles and policy, and it was evidently a spontaneous action. There is no mention of any memorial or overture from any individual or body of men—not even from any court of inferior degree. The propositions on which the Synod acted were "overtured" by her own committee on overtures. They were reported on Saturday, and made the order of the day for Monday following; and seem to have been acted on with solemn and careful deliberation. The inalienable right of the slave to freedom, the duty of the church to vindicate this right; and yet the recognition of civil society in its power, and the necessity of preparing the slave for freedom, by religious education and industrial training, are all distinctly embodied in this action. The following is the whole minute, embracing the overture, and the deliverance of the Synod, viz.:

"The following was brought in by the committee of overtures:

"The Creator of the world having made of one flesh all the children of men, it becomes them, as members of the same family, to consult and promote each other's happiness. It is more especially the duty of those who maintain the rights of humanity, and who acknowledge and teach the obligations of Christianity, to use such means as are in their power to extend the blessings of equal freedom to every part of the human race.

"From a full conviction of these truths, and sensible that the rights of human nature are too well understood to admit of debate, *Overtured*, that the Synod of New York and Philadelphia recommend, in the warmest terms, to every member of their body, and to all the Churches and families under their care, to do everything in their power consistent with the rights of civil society, to promote the abolition of slavery, and the instruction of negroes, whether bond or free."

The Synod, taking into consideration the overture concerning slavery, transmitted by the Committee of Overtures last Saturday, came to the following judgment:

"The Synod of New York and Philadelphia do highly approve of the general principles in favour of universal liberty, that prevail in America, and the interest which many of the States have taken in promoting the abolition of slavery; yet, inasmuch as men introduced from a servile state to a participation of all the privileges of civil society, without a proper education, and without previous habits of industry, may be, in many respects, dangerous to the community, therefore they earnestly recommend it to all the members belonging to their communion, to give those

persons who are at present held in servitude such good
education as to prepare them for the better enjoyment of
freedom; and they moreover recommend that masters,
wherever they find servants disposed to make a just improvement of the privilege, would give them a *peculium*,
or grant them sufficient time and sufficient means of pro-
curing their own liberty at a moderate rate, that thereby
they may be brought into society with those habits of industry that may render them useful citizens; and, finally,
they recommend it to all their people to use the most prudent measures, consistent with the interest and the state
of society, in the counties where they live, to procure
eventually the final abolition of slavery in America."—
Minutes, May 28th, 1787, p. 540.

This action is also the first taken by the General
Assembly; as we see in the Minutes of 1793, p. 76,
when a memorial having been sent to the Mode-
rator from Warner Mifflin, a member of the Society
of Friends, it was " *Ordered*, that the records of the
General Synod of the year 1787, on the subject of
slavery, be published among the extracts to be
printed of the proceedings of this Assembly."

III. The *third* distinct action was on the subject
of *communion with slaveholders.*

"A serious and conscientious person, a member of a
Presbyterian congregation, who views the slavery of the
negroes as a moral evil, highly offensive to God, and inju-
rious to the interests of the gospel, lives under the ministry of a person, or amongst a society of people who concur
with him in sentiment on the subject upon general principles, yet for particular reasons hold slaves, and tolerate
the practice in others. *Overtured*, ought the former of
these persons, under the impressions and circumstances

above described, to hold Christian communion with the latter?"

"After due deliberation, it was

"1. *Resolved*, That as the same difference of opinion with respect to slavery takes place in sundry other parts of the Presbyterian Church, notwithstanding which they live in charity and peace according to the doctrine and practice of the Apostles, it is hereby recommended to all conscientious persons, and especially to those whom it immediately respects, to do the same. At the same time, the General Assembly assure all the Churches under their care, that they view, with the deepest concern, any vestiges of slavery which may exist in our country, and refer the Churches to the records of the General Assembly published at different times, but especially to an overture of the late Synod of New York and Philadelphia, published in 1787, and republished among the extracts from the Minutes of the General Assembly of 1793, on that head, with which they trust every conscientious person will be fully satisfied.

"2. *Resolved*, That Mr. Rice and Dr. Muir, Ministers, and Mr. Robert Patterson, an Elder, be a committee to draught a letter to the Presbytery of Transylvania, on the subject of the above overture."

"The committee appointed to prepare a draught of a letter to the Presbytery of Transylvania, reported a draught, which being read and debated for some time, a motion was made, Shall this draught of a letter be read and debated by paragraphs, or not? The vote being taken, the question was carried in the affirmative. The consideration of the draught was resumed, and after very considerable time spent therein, it was amended and adopted, and ordered to be signed, and sent to the Presbytery of Transylvania by their Commissioners."—*Minutes*, 1795, pp. 103, 104.

The Letter.

"To our brethren, members of the Presbyterian Church, under the
care of Transylvania Presbytery.

DEAR FRIENDS AND BRETHREN:—The General Assembly of the Presbyterian Church hear with concern
from your Commissioners, that differences of opinion, with
respect to holding Christian communion with those possessed of slaves, agitate the minds of some among you,
and threaten divisions which may have the most ruinous
tendency. The subject of slavery has repeatedly claimed
the attention of the General Assembly, and the Commissioners from the Presbytery of Transylvania are furnished
with attested copies of these decisions, to be read by the
Presbytery when it shall appear to them proper, together
with a copy of this letter, to the several Churches under
their care.

'The General Assembly have taken every step which
they deemed expedient or wise, to encourage emancipation, and to render the state of those who are in slavery as
mild and tolerable as possible.

"Forbearance and peace are frequently inculcated and
enjoined in the New Testament: 'Blessed are the peace-
makers:' 'Let no one do anything through strife and
vain-glory:' 'Let each esteem others better than himself.'
The followers of Jesus ought conscientiously to walk worthy of their vocation, 'with all lowliness and meekness,
with long-suffering, forbearing one another, endeavouring
to keep the unity of the Spirit in the bond of peace.' If
every difference of opinion were to keep men at a distance,
they could subsist in no state of society, either civil or religious. The General Assembly would impress this upon
the minds of their brethren, and urge them to follow peace,
and the things which make for peace.

"The General Assembly commend our dear friends and
brethren to the grace of God, praying that the peace of

God, which passeth all understanding, may possess their hearts and minds.

"Signed by order of the Assembly."—*Minutes*, 1795, p. 104.

The original draught of this letter has been judiciously preserved for us by the Editor of the Board of Publication; and it appears from a foot-note, on page 104, that, in the course of the discussion, large paragraphs, fully half of the whole paper, were stricken out. One of these, it may well comport with our object to insert here, as showing the mind of the Church in what she would not declare; either because it had been already declared substantially, or because its forms of expression were objectionable.

"The General Assembly earnestly recommend to all under the care of any of their Presbyteries, who may be in possession of slaves, to make conscience to bring all of them up in the nurture and admonition of the Lord; to have them taught to read; to impress their minds with the importance of Christianity; and to familiarize them to habits of industry and order. A neglect of this is inconsistent with the character of a Christian master; but the observance might prevent, in great part, what is really the moral evil attending slavery; namely, allowing precious souls under the charge of masters to perish for lack of knowledge. Freedom is desirable, but it cannot at all times be enjoyed with advantage; a parent, to set his child loose from all authority, would be doing him the most essential injury. The child must first be prepared by education and discipline to act for himself, before the restraint of parental authority is taken off. A slave let loose upon society, ignorant, idle, and headstrong, is in a state to injure others, and to ruin himself. No Christian master can answer for such conduct to his own mind. The slave must first be in a situation to act properly as a member of civil society, before he can advantageously be introduced therein."

IV. *The Brotherhood* of all the races in our country, free and slave, civilized and savage, distinguished every plan of benevolence, in the Presbyterian Church, *at the opening of the present century.* "The gospelizing of the Indians—with a plan for their civilization," "*the instruction of the negroes,* the poor, and those who are destitute of the means of grace"—are the great objects proposed by our General Assembly in 1800, when the system was first projected, that has now been matured into five or six different departments of effective beneficence. See *Minutes,* 1800, pp. 195, 206; also, of 1801, p. 228.

In 1801, it was *resolved,* that " Mr. John Chavis, a black man of prudence and piety, who has been educated and licensed to preach by the Presbytery of Lexington, in Virginia, be employed as a missionary among the people of his own colour, until the meeting of the next General Assembly. And that for his better direction in the discharge of duties, which are attended with many circumstances of delicacy and difficulty, some prudential instructions be issued to him by the Assembly, governing himself by which the knowledge of religion among that people may be made more and more to strengthen the order of society. And the Rev. Messrs. Hoge, Alexander, Logan, and Stephenson, were appointed a committee to draught instructions to said Chavis, and prescribe his route."—*Minutes*, p. 229.

This black missionary, it is said, continued in the service, thus directed, several years.

In 1807, the Presbytery of Union sent an overture to the General Assembly, for advice in the case of John Gloucester, a black man, who had been preparing for the ministry, under their direction, but was not yet qualified, in the usual attainments— while the need for his services was loud and urgent. In answer, it was *Resolved*, 1st, That the General Assembly highly approve the caution and prudence of the Presbytery of Union in this case. 2d, That, considering the circumstances of this particular case, viz. the evidence of unusual talents, discretion, and piety, possessed by John Gloucester; the good reason there is to believe that he may be highly useful in preaching the gospel among those of his own colour; and the various difficulties likely to attend a farther delay in proceeding in this case, the General Assembly did, and hereby do, authorize the Presbytery of Philadelphia to consider the case of John

2

Gloucester; and, if they think proper, to license him
to preach the gospel." See *Minutes*, 1807, p. 381.

That this black brother was approved in the ministry, and in the highest ecclesiastical fellowship
with his white brethren, is evident from the fact,
that he had a seat in the General Assembly of 1817,
as a regular member, and commissioner from the
Presbytery of Philadelphia.

In 1815, the General Assembly began to *rebuke
the buying and selling of slaves, and all cruelty of treatment*—while at the same time reiterating the importance of preparing the slave for liberty, by careful
education.

"The committee to which was committed the report of
the committee to which the petition of some Elders, who
entertain conscientious scruples on the subject of holding
slaves, together with that of the Synod of Ohio, concerning the buying and selling of slaves, had been referred, reported, and their report being read and amended, is as
follows, viz.:

"The General Assembly have repeatedly declared their
cordial approbation of those principles of civil liberty
which appear to be recognised by the Federal and State
governments in these United States. They have expressed
their regret that the slavery of the Africans, and of their
descendants, still continues in so many places, and even
among those within the pale of the Church, and have
urged the Presbyteries under their care to adopt such
measures as will secure at least to the rising generation of
slaves, within the bounds of the Church, a religious education, that they may be prepared for the exercise and enjoyment of liberty, when God in his providence may open
a door for their emancipation. The committee refer said

petitioners to the printed extracts of the Synod of New York and Philadelphia, for the year 1787, on this subject, republished by the Assembly in 1793, and also to the extracts of the Minutes of the Assembly for 1795, which last are in the following words, viz. [See above.]

"This is deemed a sufficient answer to the first petition, and with regard to the second, the Assembly observe, that although in some sections of our country, under certain circumstances, the transfer of slaves may be unavoidable, yet they consider the buying and selling of slaves by way of traffic, and all undue severity in the management of them, as inconsistent with the spirit of the gospel. And they recommend it to the Presbyteries and Sessions under their care, to make use of all prudent measures to prevent such shameful and unrighteous conduct."—*Minutes*, 1815, p. 585.

Again, in approving promptly and heartily the organization of the American Colonization Society, which took place in December, 1816, and which the General Assembly has recommended no less than *eleven* times, more or less directly, from 1817 to 1853, we find the most emphatic recognition of the black man as a brother, whose degradation is deplored, and whose elevation to liberty and equality is to be attempted, by every legitimate means.

Thus in 1819, the Assembly said—"The situation of the people of colour in this country has frequently attracted the attention of this Assembly. In the distinctive and indelible marks of their colour, and the prejudices of the people, an insuperable obstacle has been placed to the execution of any plan for elevating their character, and placing them on a

footing with their brethren of the same common
family. In restoring them to the land of their
fathers, the Assembly hope that the way may be
opened, not only for the accomplishment of that object, but for introducing civilization and the gospel
to the benighted nations of Africa. From the in-
formation and statements received, the Assembly believe that the proposed colony in Africa may be
made a powerful auxiliary in the efforts which are
making to abolish the iniquitous traffic in slaves
carried on in Africa, and happily calculated to lay
the foundation of a gradual emancipation of slaves
in our own country, in a legal and constitutional
manner, and without violating the rights or injuring
the feelings of our southern brethren. With these
views the Assembly feel it a duty to recommend the
American Society for colonizing the free people of
colour of the United States to the patronage and attention of the churches under their care, and to be-
nevolent individuals throughout the Union."—*Minutes* of 1819, p. 710.

V. *The complete summary of principles and direc-
tions, given, once for all, in the Act of* 1818.

No other branch of the church on this continent,
even the most local in its occupation, North or
South, and much less any other one cöextensive
with the whole territory of the nation, and repre-
senting all the diversities of social life in the land,
has a record so early, and so explicit, and so ample,

as this one, upon the subject of slavery. It was made, too, at the very point, in time, of the divergence between the North and the South, which brought upon our country the struggle that has continued ever since, with greater or less demonstration of animosity. Missouri had applied in 1817 for leave to make a Constitution, with a view to admission as a State of the Union; and the extension of slavery into new States, was the great question which awakened the most profound solicitude among patriots and Christians. It was a time of memorable excitement in the political world—so great as even then to threaten the disruption of this Republic. We may well, therefore, admire the unanimity with which the Presbyterian Church adopted the calm, fair, full and fearless deliverance, which is as follows:

(a) "The following resolution was submitted to the Assembly, viz.

"*Resolved*, That a person who shall sell as a slave, a member of the church, who shall be at the time in good standing in the church and unwilling to be sold, acts inconsistently with the spirit of Christianity; and ought to be debarred from the communion of the church.

"After considerable discussion, the subject was committed to Dr. Green, Dr. Baxter, and Mr. Burgess, to prepare a.report to be adopted by the Assembly, embracing the object of the above resolution, and also expressing the opinion of the Assembly in general, as to slavery."—*Minutes*, 1818, p. 688.

[The report of the committee was unanimously adopted, and is as follows, viz.]

2 *

"The General Assembly of the Presbyterian Church, having taken into consideration the subject of slavery, think proper to make known their sentiments upon it to the churches and people under their care.

(b) "We consider the voluntary enslaving of one portion of the human race by another, as a gross violation of the most precious and sacred rights of human nature; as utterly inconsistent with the law of God, which requires us to love our neighbour as ourselves, and as totally irreconcilable with the spirit and principles of the gospel of Christ, which enjoin that 'all things whatsoever ye would that men should do to you, do ye even so to them.' Slavery creates a paradox in the moral system; it exhibits rational, accountable, and immortal beings in such circumstances as scarcely to leave them the power of moral action. It exhibits them as dependent on the will of others, whether they shall receive religious instruction; whether they shall know and worship the true God; whether they shall enjoy the ordinances of the gospel; whether they shall perform the duties and cherish the endearments of husbands and wives, parents and children, neighbours and friends; whether they shall preserve their chastity and purity, or regard the dictates of justice and humanity. Such are some of the consequences of slavery—consequences not imaginary, but which connect themselves with its very existence. The evils to which the slave is always exposed often take place in fact, and in their very worst degree and form; and where all of them do not take place, as we rejoice to say in many instances, through the influence of the principles of humanity and religion on the mind of masters, they do not—still the slave is deprived of his natural right, degraded as a human being, and exposed to the danger of passing into the hands of a master who may inflict upon him all the hardships and injuries which inhumanity and avarice may suggest.

" From this view of the consequences resulting from the

practice into which Christian people have most inconsistently fallen, of enslaving a portion of their brethren of mankind—for 'God hath made of one blood all nations of men to dwell on the face of the earth,'—it is manifestly the duty of all Christians who enjoy the light of the present day, when the inconsistency of slavery, both with the dictates of humanity and religion, has been demonstrated, and is generally seen and acknowledged, to use their honest, earnest, and unwearied endeavours, to correct the errors of former times, and as speedily as possible to efface this blot on our holy religion, and to obtain the complete abolition of slavery throughout Christendom, and if possible throughout the world.

(c) "We rejoice that the Church to which we belong commenced as early as any other in this country, the good work of endeavouring to put an end to slavery, and that in the same work many of its members have ever since been, and now are, among the most active, vigorous, and efficient labourers. We do, indeed, tenderly sympathize with those portions of our Church and our country where the evil of slavery has been entailed upon them ; where a great, and the most virtuous part of the community abhor slavery, and wish its extermination as sincerely as any others—but where the number of slaves, their ignorance, and their vicious habits generally, render an immediate and universal emancipation inconsistent alike with the safety and happiness of the master and the slave. With those who are thus circumstanced, we repeat that we tenderly sympathize. At the same time, we earnestly exhort them to continue, and if possible, to increase their exertions to effect a total abolition of slavery. We exhort them to suffer no greater delay to take place in this most interesting concern, than a regard to the public welfare truly and indispensably demands.

(d) "As our country has inflicted a most grievous injury upon the unhappy Africans, by bringing them into slavery,

we cannot indeed urge that we should add a second injury
to the first, by emancipating them in such manner as that
they will be likely to destroy themselves or others.   But
we do think that our country ought to be governed in this
matter by no other consideration than an honest and impartial regard to the happiness of the injured party, uninfluenced by the expense or inconvenience which such a regard may involve.   We, therefore, warn all who belong to
our denomination of Christians, against unduly extending
this plea of necessity; against making it a cover for the
love and practice of slavery, or a pretence for not using
efforts that are lawful and practicable, to extinguish this
evil.

"And we, at the same time, exhort others to forbear
harsh censures, and uncharitable reflections on their brethren, who unhappily live among slaves whom they cannot
immediately set free; but who, at the same time, are really
using all their influence, and all their endeavours, to bring
them into a state of freedom, as soon as a door for it can
be safely opened.

"Having thus expressed our views of slavery, and of
the duty indispensably incumbent on all Christians to
labour for its complete extinction, we proceed to recommend, and we do it with all the earnestness and solemnity
which this momentous subject demands, a particular attention to the following points:

(c) "We recommend to all our people to patronize and
encourage the Society lately formed, for colonizing in Africa, the land of their ancestors, the free people of colour
in our country.   We hope that much good may result from
the plans and efforts of this Society.   And while we exceedingly rejoice to have witnessed its origin and organization among the holders of slaves, as giving an unequivocal
pledge of their desires to deliver themselves and their
country from the calamity of slavery; we hope that those
portions of the American union, whose inhabitants are by

a gracious providence more favourably circumstanced, will cordially, and liberally, and earnestly co-operate with their brethren, in bringing about the great end contemplated.

(ƒ) "We recommend to all the members of our religious denomination, not only to permit, but to facilitate and encourage the instruction of their slaves in the principles and duties of the Christian religion; by granting them liberty to attend on the preaching of the gospel, when they have opportunity; by favouring the instruction of them in the Sabbath-school, wherever those schools can be formed; and by giving them all other proper advantages for acquiring the knowledge of their duty both to God and to man. We are perfectly satisfied, that it is incumbent on all Christians to communicate religious instruction to those who are under their authority, so that the doing of this in the case before us, so far from operating, as some have apprehended that it might, as an incitement to insubordination and insurrection, would, on the contrary, operate as the most powerful means for the prevention of those evils.

(g) "We enjoin it on all Church Sessions and Presbyteries, under the care of this Assembly, to discountenance, and as far as possible to prevent, all cruelty of whatever kind in the treatment of slaves: especially the cruelty of separating husband and wife, parents and children, and that which consists in selling slaves to those who will either themselves deprive these unhappy people of the blessings of the gospel, or who will transport them to places where the gospel is not proclaimed, or where it is forbidden to slaves to attend upon its institutions. And if it shall ever happen that a Christian professor in our communion shall sell a slave who is also in communion and good standing with our Church, contrary to his or her will and inclination, it ought immediately to claim the particular attention of the proper Church judicature; and unless there be such peculiar circumstances attending the case as can but seldom happen, it ought to be followed, without delay, by a suspension of the offender from all the privileges of the Church till he repent, and make all the reparation in his power to the injured party."—*Minutes*, 1818, p. 692.

From 1818 to 1835 this clear and comprehensive declaration of the church, so unanimously adopted, seemed to settle the question; and we find no farther action on the records, excepting notices of good success in the religious instruction of the slaves, till this latter year 1835, when the increasing agitation over the country, and the importunity of memorialists, led the Assembly to appoint a committee, to whom all papers on the subject should be referred, and who were instructed to report to the next General Assembly. This committee consisted of "Dr. Miller, Dr. Beman, Dr. Hoge, Mr. Dickey and Mr. Witherspoon."

In 1836, the committee reported accordingly; and offered a brief paper for adoption by the Assembly—to the purport, that slavery was so much a civil institution, and a subject of so intense an agitation, on which churches represented in the Assembly were so greatly divided, and in acting on which so little benefit could enure to the slaves themselves, that "it was not expedient for the Assembly to take any further order in relation to this subject."

The Rev. James H. Dickey submitted a minority report of great length, in which it was urgently declared, that a dangerous change of views, since 1818, had been coming into the Church, that slavery "begins to claim a lodgment, not by indulgence merely, but as of right;" and after portraying the evils, the encroachments, and the perils of the system, both to church and state, called on the Assembly to denounce it as a " heinous sin," to be censured by the church, and to be abandoned by every Christian entangled, " without delay."

Both these reports were spread at full length on the Minutes, and were made the order of the day for Monday, a full week after. When the order was called, Mr. McElhenny, of Lexington Presbytery, Va., moved to postpone both reports, and offered as a substitute the following : " Whereas, the subject of Slavery is inseparably connected with the laws of many States of this Union, in which it exists under the sanction of said laws, and of the Constitution of the United States;—And, whereas, Slavery is recognised in both the Old and New Testament as an existing relation, and is not condemned by the authority of God, therefore, *Resolved*, That the General Assembly have no authority to assume or exercise jurisdiction in regard to the existence of Slavery." While this motion was under consideration, Dr. James Hoge moved an indefinite postponement of the whole subject, which was carried, by a vote of 154 yeas, to 87 nays, and 4 who declined voting. The form of this motion is as follows :

" Inasmuch as the Constitution of the Presbyterian Church, in its preliminary and fundamental principles, declares that no Church judicatory ought to pretend to make

laws, to bind the conscience, in virtue of their own authority: and as the urgency of the business of the Assembly,
and the shortness of the time during which they can continue in session, render it impossible to deliberate and decide judiciously on the subject of slavery in its relations to
the Church ; therefore, resolved, that this whole subject be
indefinitely postponed."—*Minutes*, 1836, pp. 247, 248, 272,
273.

This resolute postponement, the convulsion of that
Old and New School controversy on doctrine and
policy, which now submerged all other agitations,
the compact and homogeneous feeling which resulted
from the separation that ensued, and the energy
with which the Church girded herself anew for the
apostolic responsibilities upon her, all contributed to
give unity and rest in the Presbyterian Church
for nine years; while nearly all other evangelical
churches were falling to pieces over the question of
slavery.

The reproach of *ultra conservatism*, cast upon the
Old School, is unfair. The first deliberate and de-
termined postponement of action on Slavery, as we
here see, was by an Assembly in which the New
School influence predominated—that of 1836. But
this was by no means a party vote: and neither
branch of the Presbyterian Church ever shunned
the responsibility of meeting the question fairly, at
every new phase, however diverse the tendency
came to appear, after the division of 1838. We
come now to find the Old School General Assembly,

instead of standing still upon the noble record, which was already so complete, facing new issues, and the most complicated forms, in which an overheated public sentiment, North and South, could press the vexing problem on her deliberations.

VI. *The action of* 1845, *moderating between extremes of radical abolitionism on the one hand, and pro-slavery fanaticism on the other.*

A large number and variety of memorials, nearly all on one side, with greater or less vehemence of anti-slavery sentiment, came up to the General Assembly of this year, from different quarters of the Church; and it was resolved, that a special committee of seven should be appointed to consider and report on these papers. Messrs. N. L. Rice, John C. Lord, Alex. T. McGill, Drury Lacy, N. H. Hall, *ministers*—and H. H. Leavitt and James Dunlap, *elders*—constituted this committee. The chairman was then a pastor in the city of Cincinnati. Of the remaining six, *four* were Northern men, and *two* Southern. After long and careful consultation, the following report was submitted, and adopted by the Assembly :

"The committee to whom were referred the memorials on the subject of slavery, beg leave to submit the following report:

(*a*) "The memorialists may be divided into three classes, viz.

" 1. Those which represent the system of slavery, as it exists in these United States, as a great evil, and pray this

3

General Assembly to adopt measures for the amelioration of the condition of the slaves.

" 2. Those which ask the Assembly to receive memorials on the subject of slavery, to allow a full discussion of it, and to enjoin upon the members of our Church, residing in States whose laws forbid the slaves being taught to read, to seek by all lawful means the repeal of those laws.

" 3. Those which represent slavery as a moral evil, a heinous sin in the sight of God, calculated to bring upon the Church the curse of God, and calling for the exercise of discipline in the case of those who persist in maintaining or justifying the relation of master to slaves.

(*b*) "The question which is now unhappily agitating and dividing other branches of the Church, and which is pressed upon the attention of the Assembly by one of the three classes of memorialists just named, is, whether the holding of slaves is, under all circumstances, a heinous sin, calling for the discipline of the Church.

(*c*) "The Church of Christ is a spiritual body, whose jurisdiction extends to the religious faith and moral conduct of her members. She cannot legislate, where Christ has not legislated, nor make terms of membership which he has not made. The question, therefore, which this Assembly is called to decide, is this : Do the Scriptures teach that the holding of slaves, without regard to circumstances, is a sin, the renunciation of which should be made a condition of membership in the Church of Christ?

(*d*) "It is impossible to answer this question in the affirmative, without contradicting some of the plainest declarations of the word of God. That slavery existed in the days of Christ and his apostles is an admitted fact. That they did not denounce the relation itself as sinful, as inconsistent with Christianity : that slaveholders were admitted to membership in the churches organized by the apostles ; that whilst they were required to treat their slaves with kindness, and as rational, accountable, immortal beings, and, if Christians, as brethren in the Lord, they were not commanded to emancipate them ; that slaves were required to be 'obedient to their masters according to the flesh, with fear and trembling, with singleness of heart as unto Christ,' are facts which meet the eye of every reader of the New Testament. This Assembly cannot, therefore, denounce the holding of slaves as necessarily a heinous and scandalous sin, calculated to bring upon the Church the curse of God, without charging the apostles of Christ with conniving at sin, introducing into the Church such sinners, and thus bringing upon them the curse of the Almighty.

(e) " In so saying, however, the Assembly are not to be understood as denying that there is evil connected with slavery. Much less do they approve those defective and oppressive laws by which, in some of the States, it is regulated. Nor would they by any means countenance the traffic in slaves for the sake of gain ; the separation of husbands and wives, parents and children, for the sake of 'filthy lucre,' or for the convenience of the master ; or cruel treatment of slaves, in any respect. Every Christian and philanthropist certainly should seek by all peaceable and lawful means, the repeal of unjust and oppressive laws, and the amendment of such as are defective, so as to protect the slaves from cruel treatment by wicked men, and secure to them the right to receive religious instruction.

(f) " Nor is the Assembly to be understood as counte·nancing the idea that masters may regard their servants as mere property, and not as human beings, rational, accountable, immortal. The Scriptures prescribe not only the duties of servants, but of masters also, warning the latter to discharge those duties, 'knowing that their Master is in heaven, neither is there respect of persons with him.'

(g) "The Assembly intend simply to say, that since Christ and his inspired apostles did not make the holding of slaves a bar to communion, we, as a court of Christ, have no authority to do so ; since they did not attempt to remove it from the Church by legislation, we have no authority to legislate on the subject. We feel constrained further to say, that however desirable it may be to ameliorate the condition of the slaves in the Southern and Western States, or to remove slavery from our country, these objects, we are fully persuaded, can never be secured by ecclesiastical legislation. Much less can they be attained by those indiscriminate denunciations against slaveholders, without regard to their character or circumstances, which have to so great an extent characterized the movements of modern abolitionists, which so far from removing the evils complained of, tend only to perpetuate and aggravate them.

"The apostles of Christ sought to ameliorate the condition of slaves, not by denouncing and excommunicating their masters, but by teaching both masters and slaves the glorious doctrines of the gospel, and enjoining upon each the discharge of their relative duties. Thus only can the Church of Christ, as such, now improve the condition of the slaves in our country.

(h) "As to the extent of the evils involved in slavery, and the best methods of removing them, various opinions prevail, and neither the Scriptures nor our constitution authorize this body to prescribe any particular course to be pursued by the churches under our care. The Assembly cannot but rejoice, however, to learn that the Ministers and Churches in the slaveholding States are awaking to a deeper sense of their obligation to extend to the slave population generally the means of grace, and many slaveholders not professedly religious favour this object. We earnestly exhort them to abound more and more in this good work. We would exhort every believing master to remember that his Master is also in heaven, and in view of all the circumstances in which he is placed, to act in the spirit of the golden rule ; 'Whatsoever ye would that men should do to you, do ye even so to them.'

"In view of the above stated principles and facts,

"*Resolved*, 1. That the General Assembly of the Presbyterian Church in the United States was originally organized, and has since continued the bond of union in the Church, upon the conceded principle that the existence of domestic slavery, under the circumstances in which it is found in the southern portion of the country, is no bar to Christian communion.

"2. That the petitions that ask the Assembly to make the holding of slaves in itself a matter of discipline, do virtually require this judicatory to dissolve itself, and abandon the organization, under which, by the Divine blessing, it has so long prospered. The tendency is evidently to separate the northern from the southern portion of the Church ; a result which every good citizen must deplore, as tending to the dissolution of the Union of our beloved country, and which every enlightened Christian will oppose as bringing about a ruinous and unnecessary schism between brethren who maintain a common faith.

"The yeas and nays being ordered, were recorded."
[Yeas 168, Nays 13, Excused 4.]—*Minutes*, 1845, pp. 16–18.

The foreign correspondence of the same Assembly contains large paragraphs, which illustrate the views and feelings of that body, and were approved with equal or greater unanimity. (Committee on Foreign Correspondence—Messrs. McGill, Hope, Bayless, Sinclair, and Thorpe.) The following is extracted from the letter to the Free Church of Scotland :

"We are gratified exceedingly with the spirit of candour and inquiry which pervades your document on the subject of slavery, and leads us to the hope that we shall soon be able to acquaint our noble brethren in Scotland with the true position of the Presbyterian Church in this country.

3 *

"That responsibility for the evils of American slavery is shared by our brethren of Great Britain to some extent—that you are restrained from peremptory decision on the question of our particular duty, by ignorance of facts and circumstances, and that you appreciate so much the difficulties of our position, as to admit that a different course from that of the British churches may be justified among us for the present, are generous sentiments; and enlightened Christian moderation, which prove to us that the Free Church of Scotland is as much ennobled by elevation above the prejudices that surround her, as by a memorable exodus from the oppression that enthralled her. Could we allay excitement, and restrain impatience, and correct misunderstanding among our brethren of the British churches, we have no doubt that our course in this most delicate and difficult subject would be so entirely approved that no intimation of ultimate severance on this account would any more alloy the happiness which your correspondence affords.

" Our modes of thinking in this country have not been moulded by anything like a civil establishment of religion; by any such connexion of church and state as induces a reciprocal legislation between the civil and the ecclesiastical commonwealth. The state never interferes with us as a church, either to cherish our doctrines or to control our privileges; and she expects in return that we meddle not with her civil and domestic regulations; one of which is slavery. Every man in the church here has a political right and power. As a citizen, he has the utmost opportunity for contending against every social, civil, moral wrong, which the institutions of this country may ordain or allow. But, as a member of the church, he belongs to a kingdom not of this world, that has always been prospered in the apostolic and reforming times, by separation in counsel from 'the powers that be,' and which, while it fails not to witness against the sins of the land, would rather, as in your own illustrious example, resign even the guardianship of these powers than permit civil and spiritual enactments either to clash or mingle together.

" We learn our duty, dear brethren, not only from the peculiar circumstances of Providence in our political institutions, but from the great charter of the church itself. Here we have a religion of great principles, which it behooves us to promulgate with all possible industry, energy, and faithfulness—principles, which in the end will overthrow every form of oppression that is incompatible with the inalienable rights of man. Beyond the assertion of these principles, and their vigorous application to all the existing relations of society around us, we think it not only inexpedient, but unwarrantable and presumptuous, for any ecclesiastical court to pronounce either dogma or precept. We dare not contract the bond of union among brethren more than Christ has contracted it, nor exclude from the pale of our communion, members that merely hold a relation which Christ and his apostles did not declare, among the many specific declarations against prevailing sins, to be incompatible with Christian fellowship. Slavery existed then as well as now, with at least equal atrocity; and in our opposition to its evils, we desire to treat it as they did, rather than reduce their broad precepts to that minute kind of legislation, which engenders fanaticism, distracts and enfeebles the church, and defeats the eventual triumph of the very principles it proposes to enforce.

" Enclosed, we send you a copy of a preamble and resolutions on this subject, which we have just adopted with great unanimity and deliberate firmness; from which you will learn our determination to abide by the example of Christ and his apostles—to address ourselves, in the spirit of the gospel, more than ever, to the work of meliorating evils we cannot redress—improving a relation we cannot dissolve, and disseminating among masters and slaves that pure gospel, whose heavenly influence never fails, when free from the extravagance of man, to purify every institution which God approves, and demolish every system that is opposed to the honour of his name, and the best interests of the human race."—*Minutes*, p. 44.

Extract from the letter to the General Assembly of the Presbyterian Church in Ireland.

" You refer us to what you call ' an evil which has long disfigured our civil polity;' and submit to our consideration your resolution on the subject of slavery. We received your communication on this subject with all the frankness and kindness that have dictated your whole letter. There is no disposition on our part either to repel the counsel of brethren abroad, or evade responsibility and discussion on this momentous question at home. We enclose to you a preamble and resolutions which we have just adopted, with a nearly unanimous vote, in which you will see, that we are not contented to slumber amidst the evils connected with slavery, nor to shun investigation of our duty to the bottom.

" You are strangers, we presume, in a great measure, to the principal cause of the aggravations which attend domestic slavery in this country, such as the severity of particular laws enacted in the slaveholding States, and the extreme sensibility with which many of our fellow-citizens there refuse to receive advice, and entertain discussion. That cause is mainly the vehemence and fanatical intolerance, with which many, in what are called the free States, urge on the South instant abolition, without regard to circumstances, consequences, or even warrant from the word of God itself. We hope that a better mind, and one in accordance with the paper we send you, will soon pervade every part of our otherwise harmonious country; and suffer that ' knowledge of Christianity,' you mention, to penetrate all relations existing among us; and exert its native, free, transforming power, over every institution, which either necessity may suffer, or wisdom perpetuate among men."—*Minutes*, 1855, p. 46.

VII. *Refusal to make any further deliverance.*

Notwithstanding the clear and decided testimony of 1845, in so many different forms, memorials on the subject of slavery were sent up to the Assembly of 1846, in consequence of an impression upon certain minds, that the action of 1845 was inconsistent with that of 1818. After a due reference and careful consideration of these memorials, the following record was made, viz.:

"Our church has from time to time, during a period of nearly sixty years, expressed its views on the subject of slavery. During all this period it has held and uttered substantially the same sentiments. Believing that this uniform testimony is true, and capable of vindication from the word of God, the Assembly is at the same time clearly of the opinion that it has already deliberately and solemnly spoken on this subject with sufficient fulness and clearness. Therefore,

"*Resolved*, That no further action upon this subject is at present needed."

This minute was adopted by a vote of 119 to 33, the yeas and nays being recorded.

"The following resolution was then offered by the Rev. R. M. White, and was adopted, [without division:]

"*Resolved*, That in the judgment of this House, the action of the General Assembly of 1845 was not intended to deny or rescind the testimony often uttered by the General Assemblies previous to that date."—*Minutes*, 1846, pp. 206, 207.

As a further exponent of the mind of that Assembly, the following extract from another letter to the General Assembly of the Irish Presbyterian Church, is of interest and value. It is from the pen of the Rev. Dr. R. J. Breckinridge, chairman, that year, of the Committee on Foreign Correspondence:

"As it regards the subject of negro slavery, now tolerated in about one-half of the confederate States of this Union, it is, perhaps, due to ourselves and to you, seeing the deep interest you manifest in the subject, and the obviously erroneous opinions you have formed, both of it and our relations to it, that we should make a somewhat more distinct statement than is contained in our former letter.

" The relations of negro slavery, as it exists in the States that tolerate it, are twofold. Chiefly, it is an institution purely civil, depending absolutely upon the will of the civil power in the States respectively in which it exists; secondly, it has various aspects and relations, purely or mainly moral, in regard to which the several States permit a greater or less degree of intervention. Touching the former aspect of the subject, this General Assembly has no sort of power any more than we should have, if we met in Great Britain, over the institutions of Hereditary Monarchy, or Aristocracy, or a thousand other things, which, as republicans, we unanimously condemn, but which you, as loyal subjects, cordially approve. Touching the latter aspect of the subject, and especially as regards the conduct of ministers and members of our own church, we are of course, deeply concerned : and we beg to assure you, that since the foundation of our church on this continent to the present moment, it has always recognized and tried to discharge the duties which God, in his providence, has cast upon it, in this regard. That we have done all we could, much less all we should have done, we will no more venture to assert, than we suppose you would contend that you had fully discharged your duties, during the two past centuries, to the millions of Popish idolaters who dwell around you. What we say is, that we think we comprehend our duty, in this respect, and that, from the beginning, our church has openly recognized it and tried to perform it, both to the masters and to their slaves: and we add, that it seems to be wholly impossible for our brethren in foreign parts to understand what we can do, or should do, better than we do ourselves.

"As to the institution of slavery in itself considered, and founding our judgment upon the condition in which it has been exhibited, first and last, in most of the States of this Union; the Presbyterian Church in the United States has never failed to manifest a profound interest, nor shrunk from bearing a clear and constant testimony. If we have the misfortune to differ from you in regard to any part of the subject, of course we regret it. But you can hardly expect us to change our ancient, deliberate, and settled testimony on a subject, for a long time and very carefully examined ; nor does it appear to us to be for edification, that our sister churches in foreign countries, should steadily and strenuously condemn us in regard to matters they cannot possibly understand as well as we do, nor possibly feel in regard to them so deep and solemn a responsibility as we do. We have therefore only to say, that our fathers from the beginning, as we ourselves now, and the church constantly, have held and testified, that slavery as it has long existed, and does still exist in many of the States of this Union, cannot scripturally be made a term of Christian or ministerial communion ; and that on the other hand, it is an institution which this church never did, and does not now set itself to defend. This is the substance, very briefly, of the testimony borne from generation to generation by the Presbyterian Church in the United States of America upon this point.

"As we have already said, our purpose simply is to make a statement by which you may understand exactly how this church has always viewed this subject; you will then act as your sense of duty and propriety will dictate. We have of course no idea of discussing at large a question of this sort with you—much less of defending, in a brief letter to you, our conduct or our faith, our Church or our country, against the calumnies of ignorant or corrupt men, either in your country or ours. It is because we love and respect you, that, under all the circumstances of the case, we feel constrained to say a word on the subject; and it is because we are fully convinced of the truth of our opinions, the righteousness of our testimony, and the propriety of our conduct, that we have felt it needful to do nothing more than state distinctly our true position. For the rest, one thing is beyond all controversy; notwithstanding our unworthiness, our God has smiled on us, and has so blessed and enlarged us, that in about a century and a half he has brought us from a condition so feeble, that we had but a single minister of the gospel, to be, perhaps, the most numerous body of orthodox Presbyterians on the face of the earth; and by his grace, we believe we are more united this day than we ever were before, and as fully resolved, by the help of God, to go forward in the glorious work to which, as we trust, we have been divinely called."—*Minutes*, p. 223.

In 1848, another letter was received by the General Assembly, sitting at Baltimore, from the Irish Church, in answer to the foregoing letter of 1846; severe almost to acrimony in its tone; and yet, read and answered—the letter and answer being both published in the Appendix to the Minutes of that year. The following is the portion relating to slavery, as reported by Dr. John M. Krebs, Chairman of the Committee on Foreign Correspondence, and adopted by the Assembly, viz.:

" With respect to the matter to which the greater part of your letter is devoted, we would simply observe that we have heretofore expressed to you our position; and we would refer you to our former statements on that subject. If we have declined any further discussion with you, in relation to slavery in the United States, it is not because we shrink from any discussion of the question of slavery, or as to the question of our own duty in relation to it. We trust that we are influenced neither by timidity, nor by any apprehension that we cannot sustain the conclusions we have deliberately adopted. All that we mean to say is, that, as the subject in all its bearings is before our eyes, as we have anxiously examined the word of God to discover the principles which it discloses, as we have endeavoured to pursue a course which we believe to be not only strictly conformable to the example and teaching of the Bible, but to have been approved of Heaven, in the actual condition of slavery as it has been hitherto influenced by the uniform testimonies of our church, both in the treatment of slaves and in the progress of emancipation; and as there is nothing in the arguments you employ, whether they involve your interpretation of the Scripture, or your impressions with respect to the aspects of this institution as it exists in the Southern part of this country, or to our own relations to it, with which we have not been entirely familiar, long before you deemed it needful to call our attention to it, we do not regard it for edification to engage in a controversy, or to protract the discussion with your Assembly on this business."—*Minutes*, p. 176.

It should be added here, that in 1851, another letter on this subject was received from the General Assembly of the Presbyterian Church in Ireland,

4

and read; and a special committee, consisting of
Messrs. Leyburn, Cheeseman, Van Rensselaer, and
Martien, was appointed to answer it, "at their discretion." Still another came from the same body
to the General Assembly of 1854, and though peculiarly offensive in its expressions, was read, and referred to the Committee on Foreign Correspondence,
of which Dr. Gardiner Spring was Chairman. The
Committee recommended that this letter "be not
answered;" and this recommendation was adopted.—
Minutes of 1854, p. 41.

But the most formal determination of the General
Assembly to decline further agitation of the subject
at home, was adopted by the Assembly of 1849, sitting at Pittsburgh, Pa. It was on a report from
the Committee on Bills and Overtures; and the
minute is as follows, viz.:

"A Memorial from the Presbytery of Chilicothe, praying this General Assembly not only to declare it to be a sin,
but to enjoin upon all inferior courts, a course of discipline
which will remove it from our church. Also, a Memorial
from the Presbytery of Coshocton, asking the Assembly to
appoint a committee to collect and report to the next Assembly, statistics on this subject, and digest a plan of abolition to be adopted by our church. Also, a Memorial
from the Presbytery of Erie, asking the Assembly to alter
sundry terms and passages in the Act of 1845, relating to
slavery."

In answer to these Memorials, the Committee offer the
following resolutions for adoption by this Assembly, (which
were adopted):

"1. That the principles of the Presbyterian Church on

the subject of slavery are already set forth in repeated declarations, so full and so explicit as to need no further exposition.

"2. That, in view of the civil and domestic nature of this institution, and the competency of secular legislatures alone to remove it; and in view of the earnest inquiry and deep agitation on the subject, which we now observe in one or more commonwealths of our country where slavery exists, it be considered peculiarly improper and inexpedient for this General Assembly to attempt or propose measures in the work of emancipation.

"3. That all necessary and proper provision is already made, for the just exercise of discipline, upon those who neglect or violate the mutual duties of master and servant; and the General Assembly is always ready to enforce these provisions, when the unfaithfulness of any inferior court is made manifest, by record, or appeal, or complaint.

"4. We rejoice to believe that the action of former Assemblies, so far from aiding or allowing the iniquitous oppression of man by his fellow man, has been steadily promoting amelioration in the condition of the slaves, by winning the confidence of masters, in our freedom from fanaticism, and by stimulating the slaveholder and his pastor alike, to labour in the religious instruction of the blacks.

"5. That it be enjoined on Presbyteries situated in slaveholding States to continue and increase their exertions for the religious instruction of slaves, and to report distinctly, in their annual Narratives to the General Assembly, the state of religion among the coloured population."—*Minutes* of 1849, p. 254.

These resolutions were adopted with great unanimity. Four members protested against them, and the protest was admitted to record "without answer."

In 1850, the subject was again urged by overtures, but was promptly laid on the table; the mind of the church being now firmly resolved to try in peace what results could be gained, by a faithful application of the principles and policy that had been so often declared and so fully promulgated.

VIII. *Results* of all the previous action, and consequent refusal to agitate the subject any more.

Peace for sixteen years on the most intensely agitating subject of the age—arising from no compromise beyond what these documents reveal, was itself a grand result, to signalize that visible unity in Zion, which her Builder wills, and gloriously constructs, out of the most diverse civilizations and tendencies. But these sixteen years were a seed-time of more industrious occupation for the interests of oppressed humanity, than any other equal period of time, in any branch of the church, since the days of the apostles.

In accomplishing these results, and much more that has no record on earth, every arm of the church was vigorously exerted. The Board of Domestic Missions called to the administration of its great interests a man who had earned his eminence in the church mainly as a preacher to the slaves—the Rev. C. C. Jones, D. D. During the whole period of his energetic service in that office, immense efforts were made to reach the black population in slavery, with the benefit of that guidance which his unequalled wisdom in teaching the negro could furnish. Every number of the *Home and Foreign Record* of that time bears witness to the vigour and success with which missionaries were multiplied and money expended by this Board, under the management of that eminent Georgian, upon the fields where the Federal armies have been so recently setting free these catechumens and their children.

His successors in this office continued the policy, until it grew to such proportions, that, besides the Western Committee, located at Louisville, a Southwestern Committee was organized by the Assembly at New Orleans—an extension of work which would not have been thought of, but for the teeming plantations, to which the Presbyterian Church had now a mission of unparalleled interest—alike, in the effectual door thrown open, and the prosperity with which God was blessing the effort.

The Committees, appointed by the last General Assembly to superintend " the religious instruction of the Freedmen," already find *thousands* of the emancipated seeking instruction from Presbyterian teachers with intelligent discrimination—declining both Methodist and Baptist instruction, for that which will teach them and their children what they had been already taught by means of Dr. Jones's " *Catechism for the Oral Instruction of Coloured Persons.*" Who can measure the benefits, to humanity and liberty both, revealed in this one fact, as a fair exemplification of what the Presbyterian Church
4 *

had done, to enable this generation to rejoice in universal emancipation, without one convulsion of horror, in the savage excesses of black men, which so many had feared?

Of course, the Board of Publication, also, is now reaping what was sown so liberally, in scattering as dew-drops over all the South, so many elementary tracts for the religious instruction of the slaves—including the Catechism already referred to, and Dr. Jones's "*Suggestions on the religious Instruction of the Negroes,*" and two series of "*Plantation Sermons.*" This noble arm of our influence, for many years before the war began, had been expending on colportage alone over the South, more every year than the whole South contributed of means to the colportage fund.

By a singular providence, the first three Secretaries of this Board were brought to it from slave States, where the condition and capacities of the slave were so well understood: and the unquestionable ardour and ability of each in his office told with incalculable advantage upon the elevation of the negro. And up to the very time the war began, the present Secretary, having travelled extensively in the South, in order to comprehend its wants, and see that the resources of the Board, so lavishly expended in that direction, were wisely used, had, with the full sanction of the Executive Committee, sustained the policy of his predecessors, and aimed at even greater exertions for the benefit of black men.

So, also, the Board of Education had laboured, with similar zeal and fidelity. The Ashmun Institute is a monument of sagacious and devoted interest in behalf of the negro. For nine years past, the Board of Education has nurtured this Institution with contributions, varying in amount from three to five hundred dollars a year—not to speak of the steady favour, with which it has cherished the infant cause of religious learning on the coast of Africa—especially in the Republic of Liberia.

Thus, it may well be claimed, at every point of view, that if there be one thing on which, more than anything else, the whole energies of our church were converged for twenty years before this war began, it was the welfare of slaves in the territory of these United States; in that very way which has proved most effectual in preparing them for the great result God is working out, at present—and which this church aimed at from the beginning—freedom, with qualifications to use and enjoy it.

The harvest is now on hand. The mighty providence of God is breaking off the fetters of the slave. And what has the Presbyterian Church been doing to prepare the benighted and degraded bondmen for this jubilant change? What, in comparison with the futility of her utmost effort, if, instead of binding the sections together in 1845, she had been sitting, like the Methodist Church at that very time, to divide her interests, North and South, in final and bitter dissolution? It is not too much, perhaps, to assert, that universal emancipation, as ordered now, will escape the horrors, which had always been associated with it, in the fears of wise philanthropists, mainly by means of the inculcation, which in 1818 was ordained, and in 1845 was guarded and guided, by the wisdom of the Presbyterian Church.

Let us glean the evidence, as it came to us every year, by authority of the General Assembly. We begin with 1846.

"Another cheering token in the state of our church is the growing interest manifested in behalf of a portion of our population, which in every part of our land has been too much overlooked by Christians, in their efforts to promote the Redeemer's cause. We allude to the coloured people of this country. In the Southern States especially, means more enlarged, systematic, and efficient than have ever before been employed, are now in active operation, to diffuse among them the knowledge and blessings of the great salvation. Several of our ministers devote their whole time and strength to this department of labour, and through God's blessing with most cheering success. Nor are such efforts confined to those who devote themselves exclusively to this work: the ministers and members of our church generally have enlisted in this work of faith and labour of love with a zeal unprecedented in any period of our church's history, and which the Assembly hope will still increase from year to year."—*Minutes,* 1846, p. 222.

In 1847, the following is reported in the same way to the churches:

"In reviewing the past, we find that notice has been taken by several previous Assemblies of the interest manifested in the religious instruction of the *coloured popula-*

tion of our country. The reports received this year, justify the belief that this interest has greatly increased since the meeting of the last Assembly. Almost all the Presbyteries covering the ground where this portion of our population are found in the greatest numbers, refer to the subject, and speak of efforts to supply them with the means of grace, as being decidedly on the advance. The following are specimens of the communications we have received on this subject. The Presbytery of South Alabama say: "Perhaps without a solitary exception, our ministers are devoting a considerable part of their labours to the benefit of the coloured population. It is a field which we all love to cultivate; and to some, the great Head of the Church is intimating an abundant harvest." "Most of our pastors," say the Presbytery of Charleston, "devote a part of their time to the exclusive service of the blacks, and in some instances with the most pleasing success. A scheme is now in agitation, with the full consent of the Presbytery, for establishing an African church in the city of Charleston." The Presbytery of Georgia remark, in relation to one of their number who devotes his whole time to this work: "During the year he has been blessed with a revival in one part of his field of labour. Fourteen professed conversion, and were added to the church." Another brother, in another part of our bounds, reports " the conversion and reception into the church to which he ministers of eight coloured persons." And the Presbytery of Hopewell speak of their churches generally, as cheerfully yielding the half of their pastor's services to this department of labour. They also express the belief that several churches will soon be erected for the exclusive accommodation of the coloured people, and that the field will be occupied as missionary ground by at least one of their number, who is deeply interested in the work. Many other Presbyteries have addressed us in substantially the same language; and we record these facts as going to encourage the hope that a bet-

ter day is about to dawn upon the interests of this long
neglected class of our people."—*Minutes*, p. 408.

In 1848, the Assembly said:

"The interest manifested in the instruction of the coloured population of our country, which former Assemblies
have noticed, seems not to have declined, but rather increased. With scarcely an exception, the Presbyteries
covering that portion of our country where this class of
our population are found in the greatest numbers, speak
of the interest felt in this subject as gaining strength."—
Minutes, p. 168.

In 1849, the narrative, though unusually brief
and general, mentions thirty-seven Presbyteries,
which had shared revivals of religion during the
year; and of these sixteen were Southern Presbyteries. It adds:

"Of the fruits of these gracious visitations some have
been gathered from our coloured population. The gospel
is preached to them, and God makes it effectual. We are
glad to learn that their spiritual condition is exciting a
deeper and more extensive interest than heretofore, and
engages special labour. Several of our ministers are exclusively devoted to promote their welfare, and most of
our pastors in our Southern Presbyteries give themselves
habitually to the same holy work."—*Minutes*, p. 389.

In 1850, the narrative, though even briefer than
that of the preceding year, mentions, among the
thirty-eight Presbyteries which had been specially
revived, twenty of them Southern Presbyteries;
and adds:

"The spirit for *doing good* is the general and increasing
spirit of the Church. It has led to seek after opportuni-

ties and means: and to our no small joy we have to notice,
that our ministers and brethren manifest a readiness to en-
ter upon any work of Christian beneficence, especially any
which aims at spiritual and eternal good. An example of
this is to be found in the attention given to religious instruction of the coloured people in the southern part of the
country. Many of our ministers there have one service on
the Sabbath especially devoted to this object; thus carrying
into execution the recommendation of the last General Assembly."—*Minutes*, p. 604.

In 1851, the record is the following, viz.:

"The labours of pastors and churches in behalf of the
coloured population within our bounds, and especially in the
Southern States, have been prosecuted with zeal and energy. Systematic efforts are made for the instruction and
spiritual improvement of the multitudes of the African
race who have been placed by Providence within our reach
and influence in this country; and these efforts have been
attended with the happiest results, and with evident tokens
of the Divine blessing. The welfare of the children of Africa in their native land has also been a subject of profound
interest to our churches. The desire to give to them the
gospel, with its attendant blessings, is becoming more and
more intense, and manifests itself in the high regard and
cordial sympathy with which the operations of the American Colonization Society are regarded by the people of God
in this part of his heritage."—*Minutes* of 1851, p. 161.

In 1852, the record is:

" The Assembly notice with pleasure the efforts made to
benefit the coloured population in the Southern section of
the country. The multitudes of this class of people, from
their singular condition, as brought to gospel privileges by
a peculiar providence, constitute at home a mission field of
vast importance and of most inviting character. With few

exceptions, ample provisions are made for their religious instruction. To them the gospel is preached; large numbers of them are gathered into Sabbath-schools, and God has signally owned and blessed the labours of faithful missionaries and teachers among them, in bringing many of them into the household of faith."—*Minutes* of 1852, p. 358.

In 1853, we have the following explicit and memorable narrative:

"We must not fail, in a narrative like this, to call the attention of the churches to a subject that, for many reasons not necessary to mention in detail, is now occupying a very deep interest in the public mind. We refer to the moral and religious condition of our coloured population. Particular reference is had to this matter in many of the reports, especially from the Southern and South-western Presbyteries. It is a gratifying fact that all through that section of our country, means, more enlarged, systematic and efficient, than have ever been employed, are now using with the most cheering and encouraging success to impart religious instruction to the slaves. Several of our ministers devote a great portion of their time and strength to this department of labour. And there are not wanting many remarkable examples on the part of masters and mistresses and members in our churches, who have given themselves to a zeal and devotion in this self-denying service, that show most convincingly that it is a work that lies near the hearts of our Southern brethren, and that they are not backward to undertake. Pastors feel that the servant as well as the master is a portion of their charge. In Carolina, Georgia, and Alabama, the most of their hearers and of their communicants in a large number of the churches are slaves. The largest and most promising Sunday-schools in several of the Southern towns, are filled with coloured children, together, in many cases, with their parents, who are associated with them in receiving the same religious instruction. We allude to these interesting facts as going to show, that both ministers and people in the South have enlisted in this work of faith, and labour of love, with a most commendable and unprecedented zeal, and with a spirit worthy of imitation by all who wish the promotion of the real welfare of the African race. Let us rejoice in these things as the harbinger of a better day about to dawn on this benighted and long-neglected class of our fellow-men."—*Minutes*, p. 600.

The same Assembly, acting on a report from the Committee on the Board of Education, passed the following resolution, viz.:

" That the establishment of a high-school for the use and benefit of the free coloured population of this country, meets the cordial approbation and recommendation of this Assembly; with the understanding that it shall be wholly under the supervision and control of the Presbytery or Synod within whose bounds it may be located, thus securing such an education as shall promote the usefulness and happiness of this class of our people."—*Minutes*, p. 454.

In 1854, we have the same great history continued, in the following paragraph from the Narrative, adopted and published :

" The reports sent to us from the Presbyteries covering the portion of the church in which there is a large slave population, reveal the gratifying fact that the zeal hitherto manifested on behalf of the religious welfare of this class, instead of abating, is evidently growing more ardent and active. In their houses of worship, provision at once special and liberal is made for the accommodation of the coloured people, so that they may enjoy the privileges of the sanctuary in common with the whites. Besides this, nearly all our ministers hold a service in the afternoon of the Sab-

5

bath, in which the exercises are particularly adapted to their capacities and wants. In some instances, ministers are engaged in their exclusive service—not ministers of inferior abilities, but such as would be an ornament and a blessing to the intelligent, cultivated congregations of the land. In a still larger number of instances, the pastor of a church composed of the two classes, inasmuch as the blacks form the more numerous portion, devotes to them the greater share of his labours, and finds among them the most pleasing tokens of God's smiles upon his work. Besides the preaching of the word to which they have free access, in many cases a regular system of catechetical instruction, for their benefit, is pursued, either on the Sabbath at the house of worship, or during the week on the plantations where they reside. Thus we give thanks unto God, our common Father, that he has inspired the hearts of our brethren, in the parts of our church referred to, with love to the souls of this numerous race, and that he has opened among them a wide and effectual door of usefulness. At the same time, reminding these brethren that the work is great, and is yet far from its full accomplishment, we would exhort and encourage them to persevere and abound more and more therein, assuring them of the sympathies and prayers of the entire church for them in their self-denying labours. The position taken by our church with reference to the much agitated subject of slavery, secures to us unlimited opportunities of access to master and slave, and lays us under heavy responsibilities before God and the world, not to neglect our duty to either."—*Minutes*, p. 183, 4.

In 1855, the record is as follows:

"The prosperity granted our church has diversified and increased the duties of our church. Extending from the lakes to the Gulf of Mexico, and from the Atlantic to the Western Ocean, in a large portion of our territory slavery exists. .Nor has that people, whom the Presbyterian church found here in a state of bondage, been contemned for their degradation, nor neglected as to their spiritual interests. With scarcely an exception, the reports from Presbyteries of the South speak in Christian tenderness of this lowly, but far from undeserving class of our population, and of the efforts everywhere put forth to improve their social and spiritual condition.

"In few, if any of our Southern States, are laws enforced forbidding that slaves be taught to read. Usually, as far as among any other class, Sabbath-schools are sustained for their instruction. In cities and larger towns, the slaves have, and they prefer to have, their own churches. In rural districts and villages, our pastors devote a part of every Sabbath to their special instruction; while, on extended plantations, every facility is offered for the preaching of the gospel, and other methods of religious teaching. And we believe ourselves to be speaking the language of sober truth, when we say there are in our Southern churches thousands of slave owners, whose desire and effort is to prepare those whom an inscrutable Providence has cast upon their care, for a state of liberty and self-control they cannot yet enjoy; and whose fervent prayer is, that God would hasten the day of safe and salutary freedom to men of every clime."—*Minutes*, p. 307.

Besides this remarkable language for a General Assembly sitting at Nashville, Tennessee, the same body passed the following:

"*Resolved*, That this General Assembly has heard with pleasure of the design and practical effort on the part of the Presbytery of New Castle to establish a school, in which coloured young men of piety may receive a thorough classical and theological education, fitting them for the work of the ministry, and for teaching among the destitute thousands of this country, and the millions of Africa.

"*Resolved*, That we regard this work as an important preliminary work, aiming at the highest good of the African race wherever found; and hereby express our cordial approbation of it, and recommend our churches cheerfully and liberally to co-operate in this work of faith and labour of love."—*Minutes*, p. 277.

In 1856, we find in the Narrative, the following, viz.:

"The Presbyteries of Georgia, West Hanover, Harmony, Bethel, Tuscaloosa, East Alabama, South Alabama, and indeed nearly all the Presbyteries of the Southern country, report increased attention and success in the great work of instructing and Christianizing the coloured population, and in many instances most encouraging results are specified. In some of our churches the number of coloured communicants and constant worshippers exceed that of the whites; and delightful accounts are furnished of the conversion of the slaves. Many planters have built churches upon their estates, and employed able and faithful ministers to labour among the servants, and this work is chiefly retarded by the want of preachers. No church in the land has freer access to this very important field of Christian enterprise than our own, and it is very desirable that more be done."—*Minutes*, p. 542.

In 1857, "Efforts in behalf of the people of colour, in that portion of the country where they live in a subordinate condition"—and revivals "among the people of colour—sixty in one church in the city of Charleston being added on profession—are embodied in the Narrative, among special reasons for thanks to God."—*Minutes*, p. 48.

In 1858, the Assembly informs the churches—

"how the coloured people at the South are receiving everywhere the fostering care of our ministers and churches"—how converts were added—"including all ages and all classes of the people; the rich, the poor, the bond, the free, the young, the old."—*Minutes*, p. 303.

In 1859, the record is in the following words— brief, but very significant:

"Again, the reports which have come up to us show an increasing attention to the spiritual interests of the coloured people. From the narratives of the Southern Presbyteries it appears that the gospel is specially preached to them by nearly all their pastors. We have before us abundant evidence that the gospel as thus preached has not been unattended by the blessing of God—has been in many instances received by them in simplicity of faith, and has been made to them the power of God unto salvation. It is our privilege to state the interesting and cheering fact, that eleven Presbyteries report revivals among the coloured people, some of them revivals in several churches. One church has for eighteen months enjoyed a continuous revival; and, as the fruits of that revival, as an expression of their gratitude to the Lord for the great things which he has done for them, they have contributed a considerable sum to send the gospel to their benighted brethren in Africa."—*Minutes*, p. 554.

The year 1860 is the solitary year of the sixteen, in which we fail to find the remarkable record distinctly made.

But we find it in 1861; even after throes of convulsion had come alike on church and state. Thus we read on the *Minutes*, p. 352:

5 *

"Nor must we omit to mention the growing success referred to by a number of the Presbyteries, in evangelizing
the *coloured* people in our Southern and South-Western
States. These reports speak of increased attention to this
class, and of corresponding results. Besides opportunities
to hear the word under its regular ministrations among
their white brethren, special missionaries, in several of our
Presbyteries, devote their whole time to this class; and one
Presbytery takes notice of a particular attention paid to
family instruction by means of Jones's Catechism, among
the families of the coloured people themselves."

Such is a record of results from the principles and
policy of the Presbyterian Church, touching slavery.
The paragraphs here cited were not from the pens
of Southern men, as a general, or even ordinary
thing. Of the fifteen statements we have gathered,
all of them of course sanctioned by the Assembly,
eleven were penned by Northern men, who hap-
pened to be chairmen of the Committee on the Narrative. They are such men as Drs. Wm. D. Snod-
grass, Samuel McFarren, Willis Lord, I. S. Spencer,
Arthur Burtis, John Goldsmith, Symmes C. Henry,
S. M. Andrews, D. X. Junkin, Wm. M. Scott, and
C. K. Imbric. Drs. Wm. L. Breckinridge, J. L.
Kirkpatrick, L. J. Halsey, and P. J. Sparrow, are
the others.

IX. *The loyalty of the Presbyterian Church in
her attitude towards the rebellion of the South.*

In 1861, the Presbyteries of the South mostly
failed to be represented at the General Assembly.
Many members, of unquestionable and even ardent

loyalty to the Federal Government, thought it unwise, at that time, to take any action on the state of
the country. Hence, when a resolution was at first
offered by Dr. Spring, of New York, "that a special committee should be appointed to inquire into
the expediency of the Assembly making some expression of their devotion to the Union of these
States, and their loyalty to the Government," it was
laid on the table, by a vote of 123 to 102. Soon
afterwards it was taken up again, and made an order of the day for a particular time; when, after an
animated discussion, it was referred to a special committee of nine. Dr. Musgrave brought in a report
from the majority, and Dr. W. C. Anderson a report from the minority of the committee. This minority report, after amendment, on motion of Dr.
Edwards, was adopted, by a vote of 156 to 66; and
is as follows:

"Gratefully acknowledging the distinguished bounty and
care of Almighty God toward this favoured land, and also
recognizing our obligations to submit to every ordinance of
man for the Lord's sake, this General Assembly adopt the
following resolutions:

"*Resolved*, 1. That in view of the present agitated and
unhappy condition of this country, the first day of July
next be hereby set apart as a day of prayer throughout our
bounds; and that on this day ministers and people are
called on humbly to confess and bewail our national sins;
to offer our thanks to the Father of light for his abundant
and undeserved goodness towards us as a nation; to seek
his guidance and blessing upon our rulers, and their counsels, as well as on the Congress of the United States about

to assemble; and to implore him, in the name of Jesus Christ, the great High Priest of the Christian profession, to turn away his anger from us, and speedily restore to us the blessings of an honourable peace.

" *Resolved, 2.* That this General Assembly, in the spirit of that Christian patriotism which the Scriptures enjoin, and which has always characterized this church, do hereby acknowledge and declare our obligations to promote and perpetuate, so far as in us lies, the integrity of these United States, and to strengthen, uphold, and encourage, the Federal Government in the exercise of all its functions under our noble Constitution: and to this Constitution in all its provisions, requirements, and principles, we profess our unabated loyalty.

" And to avoid all misconception, the Assembly declare that by the terms ' Federal Government,' as here used, is not meant any particular administration, or the peculiar opinions of any particular party, but that central administration, which being at any time appointed and inagurated according to the forms prescribed in the Constitution of the United States, is the visible representative of our national existence."

In 1862, the Rev. Dr. R. J. Breckinridge offered a paper in the General Assembly, which was thoroughly discussed, and adopted by a vote of 206 to 20. It is as follows:

" The General Assembly of the Presbyterian Church in the United States of America, now in session at Columbus, in the State of Ohio:

" Considering the unhappy condition of the country in the midst of a bloody civil war, and of the church agitated everywhere, divided in sentiment in many places, and openly assailed by schism in a large section of it; considering, also, the duty which this chief tribunal, met in the name and by the authority of the glorified Saviour of sinners, who is also the Sovereign Ruler of all things, owes to him, our Head and Lord, and to his flock committed to our charge, and to the people whom we are commissioned to evangelize, and to the civil authorities who exist by his appointment ; do hereby, in this deliverance, give utterance to our solemn convictions and our deliberate judgment, touching the matters herein set forth, that they may serve for the guidance of all over whom the Lord Christ has given us any office of instruction, or any power of government.

" I. Peace is amongst the very highest temporal blessings of the church, as well as of all mankind; and public order is one of the first necessities of the spiritual as well as the civil commonwealth. Peace has been wickedly superseded by war, in its worst form, throughout the whole land ; and public order has been wickedly superseded by rebellion, anarchy, and violence, in the whole Southern portion of the Union. All this has been brought to pass in a disloyal and traitorous attempt to overthrow the National Government by military force, and to divide the nation contrary to the wishes of the immense majority of the people of the nation, and without satisfactory evidence that the majority of the people in whom the local sovereignty resided, even in the States which revolted, ever authorized any such proceeding, or ever approved the fraud and violence by which this horrible treason has achieved whatever success it has had. This whole treason, rebellion, anarchy, fraud, and violence, is utterly contrary to the dictates of natural religion and morality, and is plainly condemned by the revealed will of God. It is the clear and solemn duty of the National Government to preserve, at whatever cost, the national Union and Constitution, to maintain the laws in their supremacy, to crush force by force, and to restore the reign of public order and peace to the entire nation, by whatever lawful means that are necessary thereunto. And it is the bounden duty of the people who compose this great nation, each one in his several place and degree, to uphold the Federal Government, and every State Government, and all persons in authority, whether civil or military, in all their lawful and proper acts, unto the end herein before set forth.

"II. The church of Christ has no authority from him to make rebellion, or to counsel treason, or to favour anarchy in any case whatever. On the contrary, every follower of Christ has the personal liberty bestowed on him by Christ, to submit, for the sake of Christ, according to his own conscientious sense of duty, to whatever government, however bad, under which his lot may be cast. But while patient suffering for Christ's sake can never be sinful, treason, rebellion, and anarchy may be sinful—most generally, perhaps, are sinful; and, probably, are always and necessarily sinful, in all free countries, where the power to change the government by voting, in the place of force, which exists as a common right, constitutionally secured to the people, who are sovereign. If, in any case, treason, rebellion, and anarchy can possibly be sinful, they are so in the case now desolating large portions of 'this nation, and laying waste great numbers of Christian congregations, and fatally obstructing every good word and work in those regions. To the Christian people scattered throughout those unfortunate regions, and who have been left of God to have any hand in bringing on these terrible calamities, we earnestly address words of exhortation and rebuke, as unto brethren who have sinned exceedingly, and whom God calls to repentance, by fearful judgments. To those in like circumstances who are not chargeable with the sins which have brought such calamities upon the land, but who have chosen, in the exercise of their Christian liberty, to stand in their lot and suffer, we address words of affectionate sympathy, praying God to bring them off conquerors. To those in like circumstances, who have taken their lives in their hands, and risked all for their country and for conscience' sake, we say, we love such with all our heart, and bless God such witnesses were found in the time of thick darkness. We fear, and we record it with great grief, that the church of God, and the Christian people, to a great extent, and throughout all the revolted States, have done many things that ought not to have been done, and have left undone much that ought to have been done, in this time of trial, rebuke, and blasphemy; but concerning the wide schism which is reported to have occurred in many Southern Synods, this Assembly will take no action at this time. It declares, however, its fixed purpose, under all possible circumstances, to labour for the extension and the permanent maintenance of the church under its care, in every part of the United States. Schism, so far as it may exist, we hope to see healed. If that cannot be, it will be disregarded.

"III. We record our gratitude to God for the prevailing unity of sentiment and general internal peace, which have characterized the church in the States that have not revolted, embracing a great majority of the ministers, congregations, and people under our care. It may still be called, with emphasis, a loyal, orthodox, and pious church; and all its acts and works indicate its right to a title so noble. Let it strive for divine grace to maintain that good report. In some respects, the interests of the church of God are very different from those of all civil institutions. Whatever may befall this, or any other nation, the church of Christ must abide on earth, triumphant even over the gates of hell. It is, therefore, of supreme importance that the church should guard itself from internal alienations and divisions, founded upon questions and interests that are external as to her, and which ought not by their necessary workings to cause her fate to depend on the fate of things less important and less enduring than herself. Disturbers of the church ought not to be allowed: especially disturbers of the church in States that never revolted, or that have been cleared of armed rebels: disturbers who, under many false pretexts, may promote discontent, disloyalty, and general alienation, tending to the unsettling of ministers, to local schisms, and to manifold trouble. Let a spirit of quietness, of mutual forbearance, and of ready obedience to authority, both civil and ecclesiastical, illustrate the loyalty, the orthodoxy, and the piety of the church. It is more especially to ministers of the gospel, and amongst them, particularly to any whose first impressions had been, on any account, favourable to the terrible military revolution which has been attempted, and which God's providence has hitherto so singularly rebuked; that these decisive considerations ought to be addressed. And in the name and by the authority of the Lord Jesus we earnestly exhort all who love God or fear his wrath, to turn a deaf ear to all counsels and suggestions that tend towards a reaction favourable to disloyalty, schism, or disturbance either in the church or in the country. There is hardly anything more inexcusable connected with the frightful conspiracy against which we testify, than the conduct of those office-bearers and members of the church who, although citizens of loyal States, and subject to the control of loyal Presbyteries and Synods, have been faithless to all authority, human and divine, to which they owed subjection. Nor should any to whom this Deliverance may come fail to bear in mind that it is not only their outward conduct concerning which they ought to take heed; but it is also, and especially their heart, their temper, and their motives, in the sight of God, and towards the free and beneficent civil government which he has blessed us withal, and toward the spiritual commonwealth to which they are subject in the Lord. In all these respects, we must all give account to God in the great day. And it is in view of our own dread responsibility to the Judge of quick and dead that we now make this Deliverance."—*Minutes*, p. 624.

In 1863, a member of the General Assembly, Mr. T. H. Nevin, moved, that a committee be appointed to raise the national flag over the church in which the Assembly were sitting, at Peoria, Ill. After a motion to lay on the table was lost, by a vote of 93 to 130, a committee of seven was appointed, on motion of Dr. J. M. Lowrie, to consider the whole subject. Two reports were brought in—one by Dr. Lowrie for the majority, and one by Dr. Humphrey for the minority, both of which were adopted; the former, by a vote of 180 to 20 : and the latter, by a vote of 206 to 2.

Dr. Lowrie's paper is as follows :

"The Committee to whom was referred the resolution which proposed to raise the flag of the United States upon the building in which the Assembly is now convened, and to report in respect to the 'State of the Country,' respectfully present the following report :

" Your Committee believe that the design of the mover of the original resolution, and of the large majority, who apparently are ready to vote for its adoption, is simply to call forth from the Assembly a significant token of our sympathy with this government, in its earnest efforts to suppress a rebellion, that now for over two years has wickedly stood in armed resistance to lawful and beneficent authority. But as there are many among us who are undoubtedly patriotic ; who are willing to express any righteous principle to which this Assembly should give utterance, touching the subjection and attachment of an American citizen to the Union and its institutions ; who love the flag of our country, and rejoice in its successes by sea and by land ; and who yet do not esteem this particular act a testimonial of loyalty entirely becoming to a church court,—and as many

6

of these brethren, by the pressing of this vote, would be placed in a false position, as if they did not love the Union, of which that flag is the beloved symbol, your Committee deem themselves authorized, by the subsequent direction of the Assembly, to propose a different action to be adopted by this venerable court.

"It is well known, on the one hand, that the General Assembly has ever been reluctant to repeat its testimonies upon important matters of public interest; but, having given utterance to carefully considered words, is content to abide calmly by its recorded deliverances. Nothing that this Assembly can say can more fully express the wickedness of the rebellion that has cost so much blood and treasure; can declare in plainer terms the guilt before God and man, of those who have inaugurated, or maintained, or countenanced, for so little cause, this fratricidal strife; or can more impressively urge the solemn duty of the government to the lawful exercise of its authority, and of the people, each in his several place, to uphold the civil authorities, to the end that law and order may again reign throughout this entire nation—than these things have already been done by previous Assemblies. Nor need this body declare its solemn rebukes towards those ministers and members of the church of Christ, who have aided in bringing on and sustaining these immense calamities; or tender our kind sympathies to those who are overtaken by troubles they could not avoid, and who mourn and weep in secret places, not unseen by the Father's eye; or reprove all wilful disturbers of the public peace; or exhort those that are subject to our care, to the careful discharge of every duty tending to uphold the free and beneficent government under which we are, and this specially for conscience' sake, and as in the sight of God—more than in regard to all these things, the General Assembly has made its solemn deliverances, since these troubles began.

" But, on the other hand, it may be well for this General Assembly to reaffirm, as it now solemnly does, the great principles to which utterance has already been given. We do this the more readily, because our beloved church may thus be understood to take her deliberate and well-chosen stand, free from all imputations of haste or excitement; because we recognise an entire harmony between the duties of the citizen, (especially in a land where the people frame their own laws, and choose their own rulers,) and the duties of the Christian to the great Head of the Church; because, indeed, least of all persons should Christian citizens even seem to stand back from their duty, when bad men press forward for mischief; and because a true love for our country, in her times of peril, should forbid us to withhold an expression of our attachment, for the insufficient reason that we are not accustomed to repeat our utterances.

"And because there are those among us who have scruples touching the propriety of any deliverance of a church court respecting civil matters, this Assembly would add, that all strifes of party politics should indeed be banished from our ecclesiastical assemblies, and from our pulpits; that Christian people should earnestly guard against promoting partizan divisions; and that the difficulty of accurately deciding, in some cases, what are general and what party principles, should make us careful in our judgments; but that our duty is none the less imperative to uphold the constituted authorities, because minor delicate questions may possibly be involved. Rather, the sphere of the church is wider and more searching, touching matters of great public interest, than the sphere of the civil magistrate, *in this important respect*—that the civil authorities can take cognizance only of overt acts; while the law of which the church of God is the interpreter, searches the heart, makes every man subject to the civil authority for conscience' sake, and declares that man truly guilty, who allows himself to be alienated, in sympathy and feeling, from any lawful duty, or who does not conscientiously prefer the welfare, and especially the preservation of the government, to any party or partizan ends. Officers may not always command a citizen's confidence; measures may by him be deemed unwise; earnest, lawful efforts may be made for changes he may think desirable; but no causes now exist to vindicate the disloyalty of American citizens towards the United States government.

"The General Assembly would not withhold from the government of the United States, that expression of cordial sympathy which a loyal people should offer. We believe that God has afforded us ample resources to suppress this rebellion, and that, with his blessing, it will ere long, be accomplished. We would animate those who are discouraged by the continuance and fluctuations of these costly strifes, to remember and rejoice in the supreme government of our God, who often leads through perplexity and darkness. We would exhort to penitence for all our national sins, to sobriety and humbleness of mind before the Great Ruler of all, and to constant prayerfulness for the Divine blessing; and we would entreat our people to beware of all schemes implying resistance to the lawfully constituted authorities, by any other means than are recognised as lawful to be openly prosecuted. And as this Assembly is ready to declare our unalterable attachment and adherence to the Union established by our fathers, and our unqualified condemnation of the rebellion; to proclaim to the world the United States, one and undivided, as our country; the lawfully chosen rulers of the land, our rulers; the government of the United States, our civil government; and its honoured flag, our flag; and to affirm that we are bound, in the truest and strictest fidelity, to the duties of Christian citizens under a government that has strown its blessings with a profuse hand, your Committee recommend that, as the trustees of this church, concurring in the desire of many members of this Assembly, have displayed from this edifice the American flag, the symbol of national protection, unity, and liberty, the particular action contemplated in the original resolution be no further urged upon the attention of this body."

"The paper of Dr. Humphrey is as follows :

"The General Assembly of 1861 adopted a minute on the state of the church and the country. The Assembly of 1862 uttered a more formal and comprehensive deliverance. In the meantime, a certain number, perhaps the larger portion of the Presbyteries and Synods, have expressed their judgments on the same subject. This General Assembly is persuaded that the office-bearers and members of this church, within the Presbyteries represented here, are, in a remarkable degree, united in a strict and true allegiance to the Constitution and Government of the United States; and that they are, as a body, loyal both to the church and the civil government as ordinances of God.

"This General Assembly contents itself, on that part of the subject, by enjoining upon all the people of God, who acknowledge this church as their church, to uphold, according as God shall give them strength, the authority of the Constitution and laws of the land, in this time of supreme national peril. But this Assembly would most distinctly and solemnly inculcate upon all its people the duty of humbly confessing before God the great unworthiness, and the many sins of the people of this land, and of acknowledging the holiness and justice of the Almighty in the present visitation. He is righteous in all his ways, and holy in all his works. We exhort our brethren to seek the gift of the Holy Ghost, by prayer and confession and repentance, so that the anger of the Lord may be turned away from us, and that the spirit of piety may become not less predominant and vital in the churches than the spirit of an awakened patriotism.

"And this Assembly, connecting the experience of our present trials with the remembrance of those through which

6 *

the church has passed, does now recall and adopt the sentiments of our fathers in the Church of Scotland, as these are expressed for substance in the Solemn League and Covenant of 1643. 'And because the people of this land are guilty of many sins and provocations against God, and his Son Jesus Christ, as is manifest by our present distresses and dangers, the fruits thereof, we profess and declare before God and the world our unfeigned desire to be humbled for our own sins and the sins of the people, especially that we have not, as we ought, valued the inestimable benefit of the gospel, nor laboured for the purity and power thereof; and that we have not, as we ought, endeavoured to receive Christ in our hearts, nor to walk worthy of him in our lives, which are the cause of other sins and transgressions so much abounding among us; and our true and unfeigned purpose, desire, and endeavour for ourselves, and all others under our charge, both in public and private, in all duties we owe to God and man, to amend our lives, and each one to go before another in the example of a real reformation, that the Lord may turn away his wrath and heavy indignation, and establish the church and the land in truth and peace.'—*Minutes*, p. 56–60.

X. *Slavery as now viewed by the Presbyterian Church.*

In the General Assembly of 1864, Hon. Stanley Matthews, from the Committee of Bills and Overtures, reported a paper, which, after various amendments, was adopted "with almost entire unanimity," and is as follows :

"Overture No. 12, from the Presbytery of Newton, reciting the former deliverances of the General Assembly upon the subject of slavery in this country, and the duty of emancipation, and asking this General Assembly to take such action as in their wisdom seems proper to meet the present aspects of human bondage in our country, and recommend the adoption of the following:

"In the opinion of the General Assembly, the solemn and momentous circumstances of our times, the state of our country, and the condition of our church, demand a plain declaration of its sentiments upon the question of slavery, in view of its present aspects in this country.

"From the earliest period of our church, the General Assembly delivered unequivocal testimonies upon this subject, which it will be profitable now to reaffirm.

"In the year 1787, the Synod of New York and Philadelphia, in view of movements then on foot looking to the abolition of slavery, and highly approving of them, declared that 'inasmuch as men introduced from a servile state to a participation of all the privileges of civil society, without a proper education, and without previous habits of industry, may be, in many respects, dangerous to the community, therefore they earnestly recommend to all the members belonging to their communion to give these persons who are at present held in servitude, such good education as to prepare them for the better enjoyment of freedom.' * * * 'And finally they recommend it to all their people to use the most prudent measures consistent with the interest and the state of civil society in the countries where they live, to procure eventually the final abolition of slavery in America.'

"In 1795, the General Assembly 'assured all the churches under their care that they view with the deepest concern any vestiges of slavery which may exist in our country.'

"In 1815 the following record was made: 'The General Assembly have repeatedly declared their cordial approbation of those principles of civil liberty which appear to be recognised by the Federal and State governments in these

United States. They have expressed their regret that the slavery of the Africans and of their descendants still continues in so many places, and even among those within the pale of the church, and have urged the Presbyteries under their care to adopt such measures as will secure, at least to the rising generation of slaves, within the bounds of the church, a religious education, that they may be prepared for the exercise and enjoyment of liberty, when God in his providence may open a door for their emancipation.'

"The action of the General Assembly upon the subject of slavery in the year 1818 is unequivocal, and so well known, that it need not be recited at length. The following extracts, however, we regard as applicable to our present circumstances, and proper now to be reiterated:

"'We consider the voluntary enslaving of one portion of the human race by another as a gross violation of the most precious and sacred rights of human nature, as utterly inconsistent with the law of God, which requires us to love our neighbour as ourselves, and as totally irreconcilable with the spirit and principles of the gospel of Christ, which 'enjoins that all things whatsoever ye would that men should do to you, do ye even so to them.' Slavery creates a paradox in the moral system. It exhibits rational, moral, and accountable beings in such circumstances as scarcely to leave them the power of moral action. It exhibits them as dependent on the will of others, whether they shall receive religious instruction, whether they shall know and worship the true God, whether they shall enjoy the ordinances of the gospel, whether they shall perform the duties and cherish the endearments of husbands and wives, parents and children, neighbours and friends; whether they shall preserve their chastity and purity, or regard the dictates of justice and humanity. Such are some of the consequences of slavery—consequences not imaginary, but which connect themselves with its very existence.   *   *   *   *   *

" 'From this view of the consequences resulting from the practice, into which Christian people have most inconsistently fallen, of enslaving a portion of their brethren of mankind, . . . it is manifestly the duty of all Christians, who enjoy the light of the present day, when the inconsistency of slavery, both with the dictates of humanity and of religion, has been demonstrated, and is generally seen and acknowledged, to use their honest, earnest, and unwearied endeavours to correct the errors of former times, and as speedily as possible to efface this blot on our holy religion, and to obtain the complete abolition of slavery throughout Christendom, and if possible throughout the world.'

"They earnestly exhorted those portions of the church where the evil of slavery had been entailed upon them, 'to continue, and, if possible, to increase their exertions, to effect a total abolition of slavery, and to suffer no greater delay to take place in this most interesting concern than a regard to public welfare truly and indispensably demands;' and declare 'that our country ought to be governed in this matter by no other consideration than an honest and impartial regard to the happiness of the injured party, uninfluenced by the expense or inconvenience which such a regard may involve;' warning 'all who belong to our denomination of Christians against unduly extending this plea of necessity; against making it a cover for the love and practice of slavery, or a pretence for not using efforts that are lawful and practicable to extinguish this evil.'

"Such were the early and unequivocal instructions of our church. It is not necessary too minutely to inquire how faithful and obedient to these lessons and warnings those to whom they were addressed have been. It ought to be acknowledged that we have all much to confess and lament as to our short-comings in this respect. Whether a strict and careful application of this advice would have rescued the country from the evil of its condition, and the dangers which have since threatened it, is known to the Omniscient alone. Whilst we do not believe that the present judgments of our Heavenly Father, and Almighty and Righteous Governor, have been inflicted solely in punishment for our continuance in this sin; yet it is our judgment that the recent events of our history, and the present condition of our church and country, furnish manifest tokens that *the time has at length come, in the providence of God, when it is his will that every vestige of human slavery among us should be effaced, and that every Christian man should address himself with industry and earnestness to his appropriate part in the performance of this great duty.*

" Whatever excuses for its postponement may heretofore have existed, no longer avail. When the country was at peace within itself, and the church was unbroken, many consciences were perplexed in the presence of this great evil, for the want of an adequate remedy. Slavery was so formidably intrenched behind the ramparts of personal interests and prejudices, that to attack it with a view to its speedy overthrow appeared to be attacking the very existence of the social order itself, and was characterized as the inevitable introduction of an anarchy worse in its consequences than the evil for which it seemed to be the only cure. But the folly and weakness of men have been the illustrations of God's wisdom and power. Under the influence of the most incomprehensible infatuation of wickedness, those who were most deeply interested in the perpetuation of slavery *have taken away every motive for its further toleration.* The spirit of American slavery, not content with its defences to be found in the laws of the States, the provisions of the Federal Constitution, the prejudices in favour of existing institutions, and the fear of change, has taken arms against law, organized a bloody rebellion against the national authority, made formidable war upon the Federal Union, and in order to found an empire upon the corner-stone of slavery, threatens not only our existence as a people, but the annihilation of the principles of free Christian government; and thus has rendered the continuance of negro slavery incompatible with the preservation of our own liberty and independence.

" In the struggle of the nation for existence against this powerful and wicked treason, the highest executive authorities have proclaimed the abolition of slavery within most of the rebel States, and decreed its extinction by military force. They have enlisted those formerly held as slaves to be soldiers in the national armies. They have taken measures to organize the labour of the freedmen, and instituted measures for their support and government in their new condition. It is the President's declared policy not to consent to the reorganization of civil government within the seceded States upon any other basis than that of emancipation. In the loyal States where slavery has not been abolished, measures of emancipation, in different stages of progress, have been set on foot, and are near their consummation; and propositions for an amendment to the Federal Constitution, prohibiting slavery in all the States and Territories, are now pending in the national Congress. So that, in our present situation, the interests of peace and of social order are identified with the success of the cause of emancipation. The difficulties which formerly seemed insurmountable, in the providence of God, appear now to be almost removed. The most formidable remaining obstacle, we think, will be found to be the unwillingness of the human heart to see and accept the truth against the prejudices of habit and of interest; and to act towards those who have been heretofore degraded as slaves, with the charity of Christian principle in the necessary efforts to improve and elevate them.

" In view, therefore, of its former testimonies upon the subject, the General Assembly does hereby devoutly express its gratitude to Almighty God for having overruled the wickedness and calamities of the rebellion, so as to

work out the deliverance of our country from the evil and
guilt of slavery; its earnest desire for the extirpation of
slavery, as the root of bitterness from which has sprung
rebellion, war, and bloodshed, and the long list of horrors
that follow in their train: its earnest trust that the thorough removal of this prolific source of evil and harm will be
speedily followed by the blessings of our heavenly Father,
the return of peace, union, and fraternity, and abounding
prosperity to the whole land; and recommend to all in
our communion to labour honestly, earnestly, and unwea-
riedly in their respective spheres for this glorious consummation, to which human justice, Christian love, national peace and prosperity, every earthly and every religious interest, combine to pledge them."—*Minutes*, p. 296.

THE END.